From the Bible-Teaching Ministry of

# CHARLES R. SWINDOLL

# Releasing *Worry*
## *and*
# Finding *Worth*
## as a
# *Woman*

D0180352

LifeMaps

Insight for Living

# RELEASING WORRY AND FINDING WORTH AS A WOMAN
## A LIFEMAPS BOOK
*From the Bible-Teaching Ministry of Charles R. Swindoll*

Charles R. Swindoll has devoted his life to the clear, practical teaching and application of God's Word and His grace. A pastor at heart, Chuck has served as senior pastor to congregations in Texas, Massachusetts, and California. He currently pastors Stonebriar Community Church in Frisco, Texas, but Chuck's listening audience extends far beyond a local church body. As a leading program in Christian broadcasting, *Insight for Living* airs in major Christian radio markets around the world, reaching people groups in languages they can understand. Chuck's extensive writing ministry has also served the body of Christ worldwide and his leadership as president and now chancellor of Dallas Theological Seminary has helped prepare and equip a new generation for ministry. Chuck and Cynthia, his partner in life and ministry, have four grown children and ten grandchildren.

Published By: IFL Publishing House, A Division of Insight for Living
Post Office Box 251007, Plano, Texas 75025-1007

*Releasing Worry and Finding Worth as a Woman* was collaboratively developed by Creative Ministries of Insight for Living.

**Writer for chapters two and four:** Sandra Glahn, Th.M., Dallas Theological Seminary
**Editor in Chief:** Cynthia Swindoll, President, Insight for Living
**Executive Vice President:** Wayne Stiles, Th.M., D.Min., Dallas Theological Seminary
**Theological Editors:** John Adair, Th.M., Ph.D., Dallas Theological Seminary
Derrick G. Jeter, Th.M., Dallas Theological Seminary
**Content Editor:** Amy L. Snedaker, B.A., English, Rhodes College
**Copy Editors:** Jim Craft, M.A., English, Mississippi College
Melanie Munnell, M.A., Humanities, The University of Texas at Dallas
**Project Coordinator, Creative Ministries:** Kim Gibbs, Trinity Valley Community College, 1991–1993
**Project Coordinator, Communications:** Karen Berard, B.A., Mass Communications,
Texas State University-San Marcos
**Proofreader:** Paula McCoy, B.A., English, Texas A&M University-Commerce
**Cover Design:** Steven M. Tomlin, Embrey-Riddle Aeronautical University, 1992–1995
**Production Artist:** Nancy Gustine, B.F.A., Advertising Art, University of North Texas
**Cover Image:** Copyright © 2009 Insight for Living

ISBN: 978-1-57972-845-8
Printed in the United States of America

# Table of Contents

# A Letter from Chuck

The Bible is full of great women. For that matter, so is history. From Queen Esther to Joan of Arc, from Mary to Mother Teresa, women have overcome adversity and lived great lives amidst trying times. Even many of the great men throughout history attribute their successes to the women in their lives—mothers, wives, daughters, and sisters. Down through the history of time march an endless succession of courageous and visionary women, women who knew who they were and the purpose to which they were called. Sadly, another group of women trudges along the same timeline, shoulders stooped, heads low. Many Christian women struggle to understand and maintain their identity in Christ, and that can lead to a variety of difficulties—even deep destruction—in every area of life.

Now, before we get too far into this, let me point out the obvious: I'm not a woman. Every step I've taken, every helping hand I've offered, and every sermon I've preached has been carried out as a man. Yet my years of experience shepherding women as well as men, raising two beautiful daughters, partnering in ministry with my wife, Cynthia, and being a student of the Scriptures have provided a number of insights that I believe will benefit you—a woman seeking to live out all that God has planned for you.

You and I both know that this world can be an unfriendly place for women. I've chosen to deal with two of the most daunting challenges confronting women in this day and age: the struggle to maintain a healthy self-image and the battle against anxiety. Chances are you've felt the effects of one or both of these twin villains at various points in your life. Maybe you have been down on yourself recently, or you have a pattern of self-loathing. Or perhaps you have been storing up anxieties that serve only to distract you from what's truly important in life. Sound familiar? These habits can become so much a part of our daily existence that we no longer notice them.

We at Insight for Living have compiled this *LifeMaps* book because of the damage these two foes can inflict in the lives of Christian women like you. The destructive results disturb both the practical realms of life and the strength and resolve of one's faith. On the practical side, the effects of a poor self-image and an overanxious attitude become obvious—engaging in unhealthy relationships, living life on an emotional roller coaster, and spending valuable energy worrying about things you cannot control.

Both of these villains have a component rooted in our faith as well. When we don't understand who we are in Christ, we lose conviction about the truth of our identity. Many cultural messages have served to confuse women about who they should desire to be, offering lessons at odds with Christian teaching on beauty, material possessions, and a person's inherent value. With this confusion comes a sense that something is missing, an anxiety for something more, and a lack of contentment with even the good things in life.

Whether you've struggled with one or both of these enemies, know this: you are not alone. It's easy to look at the ladies around you and believe that they all have everything together, that they just stroll along through life without a care. But remember: even the great women of history and Scripture had to face these foes. What separates them from other individuals is that they knew who they were and they lived in light of those truths no matter the consequences.

It's my sincere hope that as you read this *LifeMaps* book you will see the importance of rooting your identity in your Creator and Savior. May you receive encouragement from these words that follow, and may God grant you His grace as you strive to be the woman He has created you to be.

Charles R. Swindoll

*At its heart, a map is the distillation of the experience of travelers——those who have journeyed in the past and recorded their memories in the form of pictures and symbols. The map represents the cumulative wisdom of generations of travelers, put together for the benefit of those now wishing to make that same journey.*

*To undertake a journey with a map is therefore to rely on the wisdom of the past. It is to benefit from the hard-won knowledge of those who have explored the unknown and braved danger in order to serve those who will follow in their footsteps. Behind the lines and symbols of the map lie countless personal stories——stories the map itself can never tell. Yet sometimes those stories need to be told, just as the hard-won insights of coping with traveling can encourage, inspire, and assist us.[1]*

*——Alister E. McGrath*

# Welcome to *LifeMaps*

On a journey, the important thing is not speed as much as it is *direction*.

But sometimes heading the right way requires some guidance. Think about it. You would never set out on a long road trip without first making sure you knew which direction to go, right? You'd consult a map. For many people, the journey toward a deeper and more meaningful relationship with God lies along new or unfamiliar ground. They need directions; they need a map. And, even with a map, sometimes you can still get lost. When you do, it's the locals who know best — those who have been down the same roads. That's why this book is designed to be completed in concert with someone else. Wise friends or counselors can encourage us in our spiritual growth and help us avoid pitfalls along our paths.

## Using *LifeMaps*

*LifeMaps* provides opportunities for individuals to interact with the Bible in different settings and on several levels, depending upon your particular needs or interests. *LifeMaps* also places a tool in the hands of pastors and other Christian leaders, helping them guide others along a journey of spiritual growth through the study and application of the Bible.

## For Individuals

You can use *LifeMaps* in your personal devotionals to gain God's perspective on a particular area of Christian living. In addition to offering engaging chapters to read, *LifeMaps* can further your journey of spiritual growth with the help of penetrating questions and opportunities for personal application.

*LifeMaps* can also serve as a first step to healing or resolving an issue that continues to plague you. Read, reflect, answer the questions, and then contact a competent, mature, godly man or woman to discuss the topic as it relates to your personal situation. This individual can be a pastor, a counselor, a friend, or even one of our staff here at Insight for Living in Pastoral Ministries. (See page 73 for information on how to contact Insight for Living.) This step is an essential part of the journey.

## For Pastors and Counselors

*LifeMaps* is designed to guide individuals through an engaging, in-depth study of the Word of God, freeing you to help them apply the truths in even more specific and personal ways. As a vital first step in the counseling process, each volume lays a solid, biblical, theological, and practical foundation upon which you can build. Encouraging individuals to work through the book on their own allows them the time necessary for personal reflection and education while enabling you to target your ministry of personal interaction and discipleship to their particular needs.

## For Groups

*LifeMaps* can serve as a curriculum for home Bible studies, Sunday school classes, and accountability or discipleship groups. Each book in the series contains enough material for group discussion of key questions and noteworthy passages. *LifeMaps* can also foster meaningful interaction for pastors, elders, staff, and Christian leaders.

# Suggestions for Study

Whether you use *LifeMaps* in a group, in a counseling setting, in the classroom, or for personal study, we trust it will prove to be an invaluable guide as you seek deeper intimacy with God and growth in godliness. In any setting, the following suggestions will make *LifeMaps* more beneficial for you.

- Begin each chapter with prayer, asking God to teach you through His Word and to open your heart to the self-discovery afforded by the questions and text.

- Read the chapters with pen in hand. Underline any thoughts, quotes, or verses that stand out to you. Use the pages provided at the end of each section to record any questions you may have, especially if you plan to meet with others for discussion.

- Have your Bible handy. In chapters 2 and 4, you'll be prompted to read relevant sections of Scripture and answer questions related to the topic.

- As you complete each chapter, close with prayer, asking God to apply the wisdom and principles to your life by His Holy Spirit. Then watch God work! He may bring people and things into your life that will challenge your attitudes and actions. You may gain new insight about the world and your faith. You may find yourself applying this new wisdom in ways you never expected.

May God's Word illumine your path as you begin your journey. We trust that this volume in the *LifeMaps* series will be a trustworthy guide to learning and to your spiritual growth.

# Releasing *Worry* *and* Finding *Worth* as a *Woman*

## Chapter I

# A Woman's Worth in Christ

As I mentioned earlier, I am a student and teacher of Scripture and by no means an authority on women. I am a happily married husband of one wife, strongly supported and deeply loved, and the father of two wonderful daughters. My exposure to the problems women face has been limited, but my eyes have not been closed to the things I've observed, experienced, heard, and read during decades of ministry. In terms of how women have been treated, I see wrongs that need to be corrected and some long-overdue rights that need to be declared when we see the issues in proper focus. I have one major message to communicate because it is clearly in need of proclamation. And, because it is so obviously set forth in God's Word, the Bible, I am able to write about it with conviction. It is this, plain and simple: *women are people of worth and dignity.*

I sincerely hope those seven words will come through clearly as you weave your way through this chapter and the one that follows. If you are a woman who doubts her value or finds herself needing affirmation, these pages are for you.

# Humility versus Low Self-Esteem

Self-esteem can be defined as confidence and satisfaction in who we are, knowing how God views us and what He has done for us. Sadly, many women—even committed Christ-following women—have low self-esteem; they have too low a view of themselves. I am referring to an internal portrait that reflects how we really feel about ourselves. That picture has been developed stroke by stroke throughout our lifetime. The early brush strokes made by parents and family are especially significant because they provide the backdrop for the rest of our lives.

The way we view ourselves influences not only our feelings about ourselves but also our social confidence. When people feel unworthy or unlovable, they often act in ways that make others consider them so. When someone feels worthwhile, he or she will tend to live up to that image. Like our own self-fulfilling prophecies, we tend to behave in ways that confirm our feelings about ourselves. Fortunately, it is possible to realign our thoughts about ourselves so we can view ourselves the way God sees us. This takes place within the context of relationships—with God and with people.

Sometimes the topic of self-esteem makes Christians squirm. The Scriptures emphasize humility, and we may erroneously conclude that acknowledging any value or worth in our person is prideful.

It is true the Scriptures teach us to be humble:

> Humble yourselves in the presence
> of the Lord, and He will exalt you.
> (James 4:10)

> To sum up, all of you be . . . humble in
> spirit. (1 Peter 3:8)

> All of you, clothe yourselves with
> humility toward one another, for God is
> opposed to the proud, but gives grace to
> the humble. Therefore humble your-
> selves under the mighty hand of God,
> that He may exalt you at the proper
> time. (1 Peter 5:5–6)

But what exactly does *humility* mean? Consider the apostle Paul's words:

> For through the grace given to me I say
> to everyone among you not to think
> more highly of himself than he ought to
> think; but to think so as to have sound
> judgment, as God has allotted to each a
> measure of faith. (Romans 12:3)

Here Paul told believers not to think of ourselves more highly than we ought for that is pride, the opposite of humility. In contrast we are to think of ourselves with "sober judgment," according to the measure of faith God has given us. This means we must see ourselves as God does instead of either putting ourselves down or exalting ourselves.

It is just as wrong to say we are worth less than what God says about us as it is to say we are worth more than what God says. Neither view agrees with what God says. Pride occurs when we mentally or outwardly exalt ourselves above others. Do you compare yourself to one person and come out behind, or do you compare yourself with another and come out ahead? The result is humiliation or pride. True humility is devoid of all such comparisons. Many think that having a humble spirit means having a low sense of one's worth. Yet when we demean ourselves, we're actually saying, "I know more about my true value than God does." And in the end, that's pride too!

Gaining an accurate understanding of ourselves means we gauge our worth by replacing human comparisons with God's assessment of us. Who does God say we are? The woman who has placed her faith in Jesus Christ is God's adopted daughter. Have you come to grips with your position in the family of God? It's essential! Through experiencing the unconditional acceptance of God and knowing how highly He values you, you can gain courage to open yourself up both to Him and to others (Psalm 139; Matthew 10:29–31).

# God Made You with Dignity and for a Purpose

In his excellent book *The Sensation of Being Somebody*, Maurice Wagner outlined the three pillars of self-concept as follows: worth, belongingness, and competence.[1] A poor self-image relates to a lack in one or more of these areas.

In discussing these, Dr. Wagner directed our attention to Ephesians 1:3–8, 11–14, which reads as follows:

> Praise be to the God and Father of our Lord Jesus Christ, who has blessed us in the heavenly realms with every spiritual blessing in Christ. For he chose us in him before the creation of the world to be holy and blameless in his sight. In love he predestined us to be adopted as his sons through Jesus Christ, in accordance with his pleasure and will—to the praise of his glorious grace, which he has freely given us in the One he loves. In him we have redemption through his blood, the forgiveness of sins, in accordance with the riches of God's grace that he lavished on us with

all wisdom and understanding. . . .
In him we were also chosen, having
been predestined according to the plan
of him who works out everything in
conformity with the purpose of his will,
in order that we, who were the first to
hope in Christ, might be for the praise
of his glory. And you also were included
in Christ when you heard the word of
truth, the gospel of your salvation. Having believed, you were marked in him
with a seal, the promised Holy Spirit,
who is a deposit guaranteeing our
inheritance until the redemption of
those who are God's possession—to the
praise of his glory. (NIV)

Dr. Wagner demonstrated from this passage how our relationship with God provides for all three areas needed for a healthy self-concept. All three persons of the Trinity are connected to specific needs each meets for us.

1. We experience belongingness with the Father through adoption as sons into His family. (Even though the text addresses both males and females, Paul described "adoption as sons" because in his day sons received a better inheri- tance than daughters. The point is not gender; the point is the lavish benefits of the Father's estate!)

2. Our sense of worth comes from God the Son who so valued us that He suffered and died on our behalf. "We accept [God's] forgiveness and regard ourselves as righteous because of His grace. . . . We can regard ourselves as guiltless. This is the basis for a true sense of worthiness."[2]

3.  A sense of competence is found in the Holy Spirit, who enables us to accomplish worthwhile things. The Spirit of God also seals us, thus providing security in the family of God.[3]

Humans are worth more than the whole world because of Jesus's blood. We're also precious to God as His own adopted children. In fact, as a believer in Christ you belong to a heavenly family twice over. First, you were made by the Creator as His own possession. Then, you were bought out of the slave market of sin and adopted, chosen by the Father. And now, the Holy Spirit assures your competence by empowering you to live a godly life and fulfill God's purposes for you.

# God Values Women

Despite the wonderful truths we've just explored, many women experience feelings of low self-worth. And it's no wonder when we consider how women have been slandered:

> Never believe a woman, not even a dead one. (Old German proverb)

> Woman is a calamity, but every house must have its curse. (Persian saying)

> Wives should be kept barefoot in the summer and pregnant in the winter. (Old Deep South philosophy)

While some anti-woman messages are subtle, many are overt and brash. Add to that the conflicting messages about the ideal woman. Two extremes have boarded the ship of today's society. One extreme says true femininity means being passive and man-appeasing. At the opposite extreme is the radical feminist who applauds female domination. Both claim a philosophy that works, that offers answers to the woman who lingers somewhere between forgotten and fuming. Small wonder more women aren't confused — or eaten alive by the stress of competing voices and demands.

Perhaps it's at this point that we need to spend some time in God's Word. If the Bible does not portray an extreme picture of women, what picture does it provide?

I decided to answer that question some time ago with pencil and paper in hand. I turned through the pages of the Bible and took a close look at many of the women found there. By the time I came to the final pages, I was struck with one overriding thought. Except in a few isolated occasions, the women who appear in Scripture are competent, secure, qualified people with responsible roles to fill. By living out their sense of value and purpose, these women played a vital part in the shaping of history and in the development of lives. They are beautiful examples of humanity at every economic level of society.

Let me share with you some of the examples I found. I discovered so many that for the sake of space I must limit them to the New Testament and to just a few of the more prominent cases.

- Mary and Martha were close friends of Jesus (Luke 10:38–39).

- Mary anointed Jesus prior to His death (John 12:3).

- Many women lamented Jesus's crucifixion (Luke 23:27–31; John 19:25).

- Women visited Jesus's tomb on resurrection morning (Luke 23:55–24:1).

- Dorcas abounded "with deeds of kindness and charity" and was extremely well known in her community (Acts 9:36).

- The church gathered in Mary's home to pray for Peter (Acts 12:12).

- Women gathered for worship at Philippi and were the first to believe there (Acts 16:13).

- Lydia was a successful businesswoman who became a Christian and prevailed upon Paul and his colleagues to meet in her home (Acts 16:14–15).

- In Thessalonica, "a number of the leading women" were responsive to Paul's and Silas's teaching (Acts 17:4).

- In Berea, "many . . . believed, along with a number of prominent Greek women" (Acts 17:12).

- In Athens, some believed, including a woman named Damaris (Acts 17:34).

- Aquila and his wife, Priscilla, were often mentioned (Acts 18:2, 18).

- Both Aquila and Priscilla helped hone Apollos's theology (Acts 18:26).

- Paul called Aquila and his wife, Priscilla, his "fellow workers" (Romans 16:3).

- Paul mentioned Phoebe as "a servant of the church . . . helper of many, and of myself as well" (Romans 16:1–2).

- "Chloe's people" gave Paul information on a Corinthian problem (1 Corinthians 1:11).

- Older women were instructed to "encourage" younger women (Titus 2:4).

- Apphia was called "our sister" in the Philemon letter (Philemon 1:2).

- The second letter of John was addressed to "the chosen lady" (2 John 1:1).

Even in this limited list, you can see numerous accounts of women with purpose who occupied places and roles of strategic importance. This underscores that God never intended women to feel inferior or to live fearfully beneath some heavy cloud of unfair domination. In fact, as early as Genesis, He made a woman for co-dominion in partnership with man. In no way is a woman ever viewed in the Bible as an individual lacking in worth or dignity or competence on the basis of her gender. Look back over that list and decide for yourself.

Perhaps you have noticed a rather bold implication in my comments. The word is *balance*. In my opinion, this is one of the clearest marks of maturity a Christian woman can demonstrate today . . . living apart from either extreme and fully alive; functioning to her maximum capacity; free to be who she is and carrying out God's purpose for her. If married, she doesn't chafe at being a help and an encouragement to her husband. She has few frustrations (aside from those normal to all humanity!) connected with her lot in life or her contributions to her world, which is broader, by the way, than the fence surrounding her place of residence.

God created each woman with a unique combination of temperament, interests, abilities, and style that form the basis of relationship with Him and others. You're included on that list. And no one can take your place. God designed you to be a unique, distinct, significant person unlike any other individual on the face of the earth throughout the vast expanse of time. In your case, as in the case of every other human being, the mold was broken, never to be used again.

# Conclusion

So let me sum this up. God made you in His image. You're worth what His Son paid for you. You were adopted by the King of the universe and will inherit lavish blessings. On top of that, He made you for His own beautiful purposes to do good works (Ephesians 2:10).

My friend, it is essential that you believe the truths you have read in these pages. Believe this statement, even though you may not be hearing it from those who live with you in the same house: you are a person of worth and dignity. The word is *valuable*.

Do you realize who you *are*? Will you believe it? Will you live like it?

# My Questions and Thoughts

_____

_____

_____

_____

_____

_____

_____

_____

_____

_____

_____

_____

_____

_____

_____

_____

_____

_____

_____

_____

_____

_____

_____

_____

_____

_____

_____

# My Questions and Thoughts

## Chapter 2

# You're a Woman of Worth

### You Are Here

A female student attending her first day of seminary was listening to the professor expound on Genesis 1, where the biblical text says, "God created man in His own image, in the image of God He created him; male and female He created them" (Genesis 1:27). From her place on the front row, this student raised her hand and said, "But that sounds like woman was made in God's image."

The professor looked a little confused. "Yes . . ."

The student wrinkled her face. "But I thought only men were made in God's image. And women were made to help men."

The professor paused before replying. "No. While it's true that woman was made to help the one needing help, that has nothing to do with being created more or less in God's image. Both man and woman are created fully in the image of God."

The student blinked. Then she blinked harder, fighting back tears. "You mean I don't have to get *married* to be fully in God's image?"

"Yes. Yes, I mean precisely that."

The student's voice grew more confident. "And I don't have to have *children* before I can completely reflect God's image?"

The professor looked her straight in the eye. "Yes. That is exactly what the text says. You are made in God's image. And to be fully in God's image, you don't have to marry first. Or have children. Or do anything."

Four years later, that student had not "gotten over" the thrill of knowing the truth about herself.

This student had lived most of her life under a faulty assumption. Her struggle to understand her true value as a woman is not uncommon. Psychologist and author James Dobson wrote of a survey he did that turned up troubling results:

> *Low Self-Esteem* was indicated as *the* most troubling problem by the majority of the women completing the questionnaire. More than 50 percent of the group marked this item above every other alternative on the list, and 80 percent placed it in the top five. This finding is perfectly consistent with my own observations . . . even in seemingly healthy and happily married young women, personal inferiority and self-doubt cut the deepest and leave the most wicked scars. This same old nemesis is usually revealed within the first five minutes of a counseling session; feelings of inadequacy, lack of confidence, and a certainty of worthlessness have become a way of life . . . a way of despair for millions of American women.

What does it mean to have low self-esteem? What does one experience when struggling with . . . feelings of inadequacy? Perhaps I can express the troubling thoughts and anxieties which reverberate through the backroads of an insecure mind. It is sitting alone in a house during the quiet afternoon hours, wondering why the phone doesn't ring . . . wondering why you have no "real" friends. It is longing for someone to talk to, soul to soul, but knowing there is no such person worthy of your trust. It is feeling that "they wouldn't like me if they knew the real me." It is becoming terrified when speaking to a group of your peers, and feeling like a fool when you get home. It is wondering why other people have so much more talent and ability than you do. It is feeling incredibly ugly and sexually unattractive. It is admitting that you have become a failure as a wife and mother. It is disliking everything about yourself and wishing, constantly wishing, you could be someone else. [1]

Clearly, self-esteem, self-acceptance, and self-worth are fundamental issues that affect a woman's life. These distinct yet interrelated qualities affect almost every attitude and drive every decision.

**What external influences have the greatest impact on your opinion of yourself? What internal thoughts keep you from believing your worth?**

_____

_____

_____

_____

_____

**What life experiences have made you feel inadequate or ashamed?**

_____

_____

_____

_____

_____

# The Wrong Equations

Today's woman is bombarded with some "bad math" when it comes to worth and esteem. And the trouble is that none of the faulty equations add up. One such equation is *Appearance + Admiration = A Whole Person.* This fails to add up because we are not the sum and total of body parts or our external image.

Another such equation that does not add up is *Performance + Accomplishments = A Whole Person.* We are more than the sum total of our skills and the recognized abilities we have developed.

A third equation might be *Status + Recognition = A Whole Person.* This equation is also untrue, for we are more than what anyone thinks of us.[2]

None of these equations can satisfy with any lasting effect our needs for belonging, worthiness, and competence. Appearance, performance, and status are all pawns of circumstance, none of which come with any guarantees. And looking to them for worth is faulty thinking.

**How have the equations described above influenced your view of yourself? Which do you tend to use to evaluate yourself? Others?**

_____

_____

_____

_____

_____

Our concept of ourselves may accurately reflect our actual self, or it may be incongruous with our actual self. *Self-concept* "is what the person takes [herself] to be, or construes [herself] to be, or feels [herself] to be."[3] A person's self-concept may or may not be based in reality. A woman may have a wonderful singing voice, and people may compliment her. Yet she may believe she can't sing well and discount their comments. On the other hand, an overbearing mother may boast about herself as a good parent, but her children see her as she actually is—controlling and selfish.

**How do you respond to compliments? Do you find yourself desperately needing others' approval or rejecting positive feedback? Or both?**

_____

_____

_____

_____

When you were growing up, how did your family handle encouragement and affirmation? Did you hear mostly positive words or more criticism, negative comparisons, and condemnatory statements?

_____

_____

_____

_____

_____

If you were to base your self-concept entirely on other people's words and demeanor toward you, describe the person you'd see.

_____

_____

_____

_____

What do you perceive God to be like? How do you think God perceives you?

_____

_____

_____

_____

_____

A person's true identity comes from knowing who she is—which relates to whose she is. And coupled with that idea is her worth. We find our identity in knowing God made us in His image. And we find our worth in knowing the price paid for us. These truths are the true source of our self-esteem.

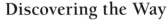

### Discovering the Way

Within the context of relationship with God and others comes the mature self—the spiritually complete person. The process of growing in Christ includes adjusting our self-concept according to our identity in Christ and becoming the person God wants us to be.

# The Right Equation

The only equation that truly adds up is *God + Me = A Whole Person*. In other words

> my belongingness is secured and reaffirmed by my love for God my Father and validated by His love for me. My worthiness is secured and reaffirmed by my love for Jesus Christ His Son and validated by His love for me. My competence is secured and reaffirmed in daily situations . . . through the ministry and love of the Holy Spirit as He uses the Word of God to instruct, correct, and reassure me; my competence is validated as I live by the Word of God.[4]

Our identity in Christ is our spiritual position as a result of God justifying, redeeming, and reconciling us to Himself through Christ's saving work on our behalf. (For more information on these concepts, see "How to Begin a Relationship with God" in the back of this book.) Our "old self" was crucified with Christ on the cross (Romans 6:6). God has made us a "new creation" in Christ (2 Corinthians 5:17 NIV). Our new identity offers a new relationship with God as our Father and with other believers in the kingdom of God.

The Bible teaches us how to have a true assessment about ourselves. As early as Genesis 1:27, we read, "God created man in His own image, in the image of God He created him; male and female He created them." What does this tell you about yourself?

_____

_____

_____

_____

According to Genesis, all humans have worth because they have been created "in [God's] own image" (Genesis 1:27). Molded by the hand of God in our mother's womb (Psalm 139:13–14), we reflect our Creator's glory as we emulate Him:

- Rationally—we reason, perceive, and create.

- Emotionally—we have feelings.

- Volitionally—we have a will.

- Physically—even our corruptible bodies will be changed to reflect His eternal glory.

If you are a believer in Christ, who does God say you are according to Ephesians 1:5?

_____

_____

_____

_____

_____

Do you know any families touched by adoption? Maybe you're an adoptive parent. Or perhaps your parents adopted you. Donald Regier, author of _The Long Ride_, described what it's like to read Scripture verses about adoption now that he's an adoptive father. "The biblical doctrine of adoption has come alive for me," he said. "I no longer view it as dogma in a dusty book. I now see it as a joyous article of faith and life. I have begun to understand this great truth from God's perspective, because a former orphan now calls me 'Daddy.'" [5] Chosen. Given a new name. Cared for. Granted an inheritance. Adoption stories are full of such words and phrases, aren't they? Add to that, "Daddy, I know you love me," and a father describing his "dream come true." In human adoption stories we catch a glimpse of what spiritual adoption is about.

**God's truth about us can guide our thoughts, emotions, and actions. What does each verse say about who you are or what you have been given in Christ?**

John 1:12 _____

_____

John 15:13–15 _____

_____

Romans 3:24 _____

_____

Romans 5:1–2, 17 _____

_____

Romans 6:14 _____

_____

Romans 8:1 _____

_____

Romans 8:15–17 _____

_____

Romans 8:35–39 _____

_____

Romans 12:5 _____

_____

2 Corinthians 1:22 _____

_____

2 Corinthians 5:18–20 _____

_____

Galatians 4:6–7 _____

_____

Galatians 5:1 _____

_____

Ephesians 1:5, 18 _____

_____

Ephesians 2:1, 8, 10 _____

_____

Ephesians 2:13, 19 _____

_____

Philippians 3:20 _____

_____

Titus 3:5 _____

_____

Hebrews 4:16 _____

_____

1 John 2:2 _____

_____

Gaining an accurate understanding of ourselves means gauging our worth by replacing human reasoning with God's assessment of us. We have worth because God has charged us with a worthwhile task—to rule the earth, caring for it as His representatives (see Genesis 1:28–30). And we have worth because God loves us. He demonstrated His love by sending His Son to die for us as atonement for our sins (see Romans 5:8). We are made in the image of God; in contrast, Jesus is "the image of the invisible God" (Colossians 1:15). God's self-sacrifice through His Son is the ultimate expression of our value to Him. Because we are sinners, we are unworthy of His favor. However, no human is worthless to God.

# Humility versus Low Self-Esteem

For decades, secular psychologists have assumed that low self-esteem causes poor behavior. So, attempting to raise self-esteem, counselors often advise their clients to "find yourself, love yourself, be true to yourself, nurture your inner you, do what's best for you." People are told to satisfy whatever their self requires and to avoid any situation that might wound the self. But those who have negative self-thoughts are already overly preoccupied with themselves. Popular methods of raising self-esteem only intensify self-focus, sending people on a never-ending pursuit to feel good about themselves—often with the following negative results:

- Increased selfish behavior.

- Damaged relationships.

- Inflated perception of abilities.

- Resistance to admit sin or permit guilt feelings.

The Bible presents humanity as essentially depraved, self-concerned, and self-focused: "Each of us has turned to his own way" (Isaiah 53:6). So rather than teaching people how to love themselves, the Bible teaches that self-love must be restrained. Jesus stated, "If anyone wishes to come after Me, he must deny himself, and take up his cross and follow Me" (Mark 8:34). The way of Christ is self-denial, not self-focus. The target of our self-denial is any part of our nature that would seek to replace Christ's rule with our selfish desires. In this method of denying ourselves for the sake of others and for the sake of Christ, we can realize the paradoxical meaning of Jesus's words that "whoever loses his life for My sake will find it" (Matthew 16:25). On the path of surrender, we "find ourselves" as we discover the purpose for which we were created and express our true identity as God's children.

**Read Philippians 2:3–4 and restate it in your own words. (Lest you think this sounds like the profile of a doormat, remember that Christ Himself, who was assertive and confident, lived this very attitude [Philippians 2:5–11]).**

_____

_____

_____

_____

_____

_____

_____

**Do you tend to do things primarily to please others or to gain their approval rather than as an extension of true humility and service? If you're not sure, next time, stop and ask God to reveal your true motives.**

---

_____

_____

_____

_____

_____

Jesus knew who He was—He stated unequivocally, "I am a king" (John 18:37)—yet He willingly chose to serve others. True humility comes only with an accurate understanding of and acceptance of the truth about ourselves.

# The Comparison Trap

Comparison is often at the heart of feelings of failure and worthlessness. This tendency emerges from a worldview that ranks people according to their perceived worth. It's imperative to see the difference between this worldview and the Bible's view of personhood.

The world's survival-of-the-fittest mentality has produced a society that worships beauty, strength, achievement, and power. When we compare ourselves to society's idols, we come up short. We feel worthless because, according to the world's scale, we rank lower than the ideal. Other times, we compare ourselves to others whom we see as "lesser," so that we can feel better about ourselves. This also reveals a low self-image.

**Do you tend to compare yourself to others? How does that affect your attitude about yourself? About others?**

_____

_____

_____

_____

_____

According to Scripture, we have value, not because we are prettier, stronger, or more capable than others, but because we are created in the image of God. Our value comes from outside ourselves instead of from our own feeble efforts at self-promotion, self-admiration, and self-love.

 ## Starting Your Journey

James Dobson wrote,

> If I could write a prescription for the women of the world, I would provide each one of them with a healthy dose of self-esteem and personal worth (taken three times a day until the symptoms disappear). I have no doubt that this is their greatest need. . . . If they could only bask in the dignity and status granted them by the Creator, then their femininity would be valued as their greatest asset, rather than scorned as an old garment to be discarded. Without question, the future of a nation depends on how it sees its women, and I hope we will teach our little girls to be glad they were chosen by God for the special pleasures of womanhood.[6]

Taking into account the truths about your worth outlined in Scripture, write a self-portrait based on God's perspective of you.

_____

_____

_____

_____

_____

_____

The Bible says you were created to do good works (Ephesians 2:10). That does not mean works save you. Rather, you were designed to function best when engaged in others-focused, God-glorifying living. What unique characteristics, experiences, gifts, and talents has God given you with which to serve Him?

_____

_____

_____

_____

Whom can you serve with these gifts? How?

_____

_____

_____

_____

People with healthy self-esteem know who they are, feel little need to defend or justify themselves, feel little pressure to perform for the sake of others, and have the ability to feel and express the full range of human emotions. What they are on the outside reflects who they are on the inside. As a result, their thinking is not "all about me" but "all about glorifying God."

Once you truly believe that what God says is true about you, you are free to accept and like yourself. And a woman who does so has the ability to love others unselfishly. Someone who believes she is worthy of compassion has compassion to give. A woman who is loved has love to give.

Do you know who you are? God made you in His image. You're worth what His Son paid for you. You were adopted by the King of the universe and will inherit lavish riches. He made you for His own beautiful purposes as the crown jewel of creation, pronouncing on you the words "very good"! And He entrusted you with a spiritual gift that's indispensable to the body of Christ. So, to sum it up, you are a person of worth and dignity. The word is *valuable*. You are too valuable for your Savior and Lord to let go of you! Embracing these truths honors the God who created you. And in doing so, you validate the fact that He makes no mistakes and that you have worth just as you are.

> *Father, I confess that my focus has been*
> *on me, how I see myself, and how others*
> *see me. Fill me with Your Spirit so that*
> *through Your power I can move my focus*
> *to You, Your people, and Your will for my*
> *life. Faithfully remind me that Jesus is the*
> *True Vine and I am one of the branches. I*
> *cannot bear fruit unless I remain in Him.*
> *Let me never forget that apart from*
> *Him, I can do nothing! In Jesus's name I*
> *pray, amen.*

# My Questions and Thoughts

## My Questions and Thoughts

## Chapter 3

# Overcoming Anxiety

As you begin to believe the truth about who you are in Christ, you'll face challenges as you put that belief into practice. One of the most insidious of these is the issue of anxiety. Anxiety is the painful uneasiness of the mind that feeds on impending fears. And it is running rampant in the lives of Christian women, causing untold destruction and burnout.

What makes you bite your nails? What keeps you awake at night? What scares you? I don't mean the kind of fear evoked by horror movies or even the daily intruders like a leaking faucet, a mound of bills, or a flat tire. I mean the relentless worries of the ulcer-causing, big-time mental monsters that crawl into your head, walk around with you all day, and steal your sleep. What dread concerns do you find it impossible to shake off? Does anything make you anxious like that?

Many if not most women rank financial strain at the top of their "worry" lists. Other causes of anxiety often mentioned include divorce, loss of spirituality, liberal views on sex and sexuality that threaten the family, concerns about both parents working, inability to pay the rent or mortgage, debt, healthcare costs, and medical bills.

While each person has a different list, deep, relentless worries have a similar effect on us. They work like petty thieves in the dark corners of our thoughts— like pickpockets who swipe our peace and steal our joy.

Left to do its insidious work, worry drains us of our resources, leaving us emotionally bankrupt and spiritually immobilized. That's why we must confront it head-on. And the first step in that process is to analyze and understand anxiety's power.

## Anxiety Attacks

When I think of what the Bible says about anxiety, my mind goes first to the relevant counsel of Paul the apostle in his letter to the Philippians. Type the words *worry* or *anxiety* into the search engine of my mind, and Philippians 4 flashes on the screen.

### What Anxiety Is

For some critical clues to the nature of anxiety, let's look closely at that first-century pastor's calming words. He wrote them in a dank, cramped prison cell to people he loved who were far away.

> Rejoice in the Lord always; again I will say, rejoice! Let your gentle spirit be known to all men. The Lord is near. Be anxious for nothing, but in everything by prayer and supplication with thanksgiving let your requests be made known to God. And the peace of God, which surpasses all comprehension, will guard your hearts and your minds in Christ Jesus. (Philippians 4:4–7)

Immediately we discover a four-word command that could be rendered, literally, "Stop worrying about anything!" The word translated "anxious" comes from the Greek verb *merimnao*, meaning "to have a distracting care."[1] The English word *anxious* derives from the Latin *anxius*, which carries the added nuance of choking or strangling. Isn't that a fitting metaphor? The word also appears in German as *wurgen*, from which we derive our English word *worry*. Anxiety threatens to strangle the life out of us, leaving us asphyxiated by fear and gasping for hope.

Jesus used similar terms when He referred to worry in His parable of the sower, which we read in Mark 4. The Master Illustrator painted in His readers' minds a picture of a farmer sowing seed in four types of soil. In that parable He described a seed sown among thorns. While doing so, He underscored both the real nature and the destructive power of anxiety. Jesus said, "Other seed fell among the thorns, and the thorns came up and *choked it*, and it yielded no crop" (Mark 4:7, emphasis added). Later, when the disciples asked Jesus about the parable's meaning, He interpreted His own words. The seeds sown among thorns, He explained, are those "who have heard the word, but the *worries* of the world, and the deceitfulness of riches, and the desires for other things enter in and *choke* the word, and it becomes unfruitful" (4:18–19, emphasis added). The Seed-planter sowed the Word. Clearly the Seed-planter, the Sower, in Jesus's analogy is Jesus Himself and His teaching. Yet the reference would also include anyone sowing truth through teaching or preaching. The soil is the heart of anyone who hears the truth as it's sown. Anxiety sprouts like weeds and thorns, grows up around the seed of God's Word, and chokes away the peace it can bring. In this lesson about seeds and soil, Jesus made a direct connection between anxiety and strangulation. Worry chokes us!

# What Anxiety Does

In its mildest form, anxiety causes us simply to churn. In its most severe form, we panic. This is a good place to pause and dig deeper. Why is anxiety so wrong and spiritually debilitating? Three statements will help answer that question. And these statements lead us to an illustration from biblical days.

*Anxiety highlights the human viewpoint and strangles the divine, so we become fearful.* When we worry, we focus so much on human events that God's perspective gets choked out. Worry strangles the divine perspective from our daily living, which puts us on edge.

*Anxiety chokes our ability to distinguish the incidental from the essential, so we get distracted.* In the midst of worrisome details, we add endless fears, doubts, tasks, expectations, and pressures. Eventually we lose perspective on what matters. Incidentals distract us to the point that we neglect essentials. Fruitful people are usually people at peace. Unproductive people, on the other hand, are tied up in knots, having allowed incidental worries to entangle their minds.

*Anxiety siphons joy and moves us from thinking critically to becoming critics.* When worry wins the battle, we take out our anxiety on others. Worry works like bad cholesterol, hardening the arteries of our spiritual hearts and clogging the flow of love and grace. Eventually, as thorns and thistles intensify, we become negative, bitter, and narrow.

We're not alone in this struggle against anxiety, and neither were those closest to Jesus while He was on earth. In the following biblical scene, Jesus, being a gentle, compassionate Teacher, offered perspective and correction to a fretting friend. We're reminded that in tough times when anxiety creeps in, filling our minds with fear, distraction, and bitterness, we can turn to the One who offers unexplainable peace.

## A First-Century Portrait of Anxiety

The scene I have in mind is recorded in Luke 10. It is one of the most intimate vignettes from the life of Jesus. The setting is the home of three of our Lord's closest friends—Martha, Mary, and Lazarus—who lived in the village of Bethany just outside Jerusalem.

Jesus chose the home of these friends as a place of refuge, an ideal retreat away from the strain of public ministry. Here He found safe harbor among people who didn't ask leading questions, who approached Him without agendas, and who accepted Him as He was. When I read this story, I wonder to myself, *If Jesus lived on earth today, would He choose my home?* While I'm at it, would *your* home be one of those places where He'd find relief?

As we consider the Scriptures, observe closely as two unsuspecting individuals reacted to a visit from their famous friend and some of His weary, hungry disciples.

> Now as they were traveling along, He
> entered a village; and a woman named
> Martha welcomed Him into her home.
> She had a sister called Mary, who was
> seated at the Lord's feet, listening to
> His word. But Martha was distracted
> with all her preparations; and she came
> up to Him and said, "Lord, do You not
> care that my sister has left me to do all
> the serving alone? Then tell her to help

me." But the Lord answered and said to
her, "Martha, Martha, you are worried
and bothered about so many things;
but only one thing is necessary, for
Mary has chosen the good part, which
shall not be taken away from her."
(Luke 10:38–42)

Before I proceed, perhaps a small disclaimer is in
order. I need to make clear that Martha's name has
no general significance. Neither does her gender. The
person who gives in to such anxiety-producing distrac-
tions could have any name and could be a man or a
woman. Young or old. Rich or bankrupt.

Martha was delighted to see Jesus, to be sure, but
when she did, she immediately realized she had a huge
job on her hands. There was a meal to cook, a table
to set, and guests to make comfortable. That required
serious planning and efficient execution. No one can
fault Martha for lacking diligence.

Luke's story offers an eloquent study in contrast.
After Martha met Jesus at the door (10:38), she must
have gone straight to work. We know that because Luke
moved quickly to describe what Martha's sister was
doing: "She had a sister called Mary, who was seated at
the Lord's feet, listening to His word" (10:39).

Understanding the rarity of the moment of just
being in His presence, Mary sat in her Master's shadow,
eager to learn from anything He had to say. Martha
"was distracted with all her preparations" (10:40). In
other words, Mary seized the opportunity, but Martha,
anxious and distracted, missed it. Martha was acting
responsibly. It was true, there was a job to be done.
Unfortunately, she was so responsible that she got
everything else out of focus.

Martha reached her boiling point and in a moment of exasperation blurted, "Lord, do You not care that my sister has left me to do all the serving alone? Then tell her to help me" (Luke 10:40).

I have a feeling she spoke those words to Jesus while frowning and glaring at Mary. Hands on hips, brow beaded with sweat, Martha likely stomped her foot in protest. Ever felt like that?

Martha's out-of-balance concerns over the meal preparations prevented her from focusing on Jesus. Because her anxiety had gotten the best of her, she missed a potentially life-altering encounter with the Savior. The stress she brought onto herself strangled her ability to relish Christ's words and experience the quiet benefit of His presence.

I love how our Lord responded. He addressed her, "Martha, Martha." Gentle Jesus, gracious and calm. He didn't deliver a thundering lecture, wagging His finger in Martha's face. He didn't throw open the family Bible and shame her into reading ten verses aloud. None of that. I'm convinced He felt compassion for Martha. He could have even wrapped His arms around her and whispered, "You are worried and bothered about so many things; but only one thing is necessary, for Mary has chosen the good part, which shall not be taken away from her" (10:41–42).

Jesus pinpointed Martha's trouble. She had allowed the anxiety of the moment to cloud her attitude, rob her of right priorities, and steal her joy. Often that twisted mind-set shows up plain as day on our grimacing faces. I wonder if Martha's body language betrayed her internal stress.

Mary had chosen a better way—the way of life and peace found at the feet of Jesus. For the rest of her life she would be able to remember those precious hours with her beloved Savior. Martha may have known only frustration and regret had not Jesus lovingly rebuked her.

# The Dynamics of Anxiety

After years of studying anxiety (and yielding to it too often), I've distilled what I've learned about its destructive power into four principles. They may seem negative at first glance, but when embraced and acted on, they can become powerful antidotes against anxiety's sting. They're crafted in terms of simple math—addition, subtraction, multiplication, and division. I'd like to share them with you.

*We worry when we* add *unnecessary pressure to an already full plate.* This is the most common error busy people make. It's the addition that defeats us! We worry when we add the pressure of exterior image, when we increase the pace to keep up with the Joneses, when we intensify our emotional responsibility in response to someone else's struggle. We worry when we take responsibility to fulfill the unreasonable expectations of others. I've personally struggled with that one over the years. As a pastor, I used to worry about living up to the expectations of so many people. What a terrible way to live or to minister! Trying to meet everyone's expectations adds unnecessary pressure. So you and I worry when we add things to a plate of cares already full.

*We worry when we* subtract *God's presence from our crises.* We worry when we forget God's presence and God's sovereignty. We worry when we subtract His timing from our plans. When we eliminate prayer from our daily routines. When we subtract divine perspective from tough times. Anxiety overcomes us when we subtract God's infinite power from our own feeble initiatives.

The late Peter Marshall, renowned chaplain of the United States Senate, prayed,

> Father . . . Check our impulse to spread
> ourselves so thin that we are exposed
> to fear and doubt, to the weariness and
> impatience that makes our tempers
> wear thin, that robs us of peace of
> mind, that makes skies gray when they
> should be blue, that stifles a song along
> the corridors of our heart.[2]

The seasoned pastor understood that adversity minus God's presence equals doubt and fear. Every time. Subtracting makes us doubtful.

*We worry when we* multiply *our problems by inserting solutions prematurely.* When we insert our solutions too rapidly, complications set in. And then we worry when our so-called solutions fail. Anxiety grips us when we insist on finding a way out of the tough stretches in life instead of taking God's path through them. We rush ahead of Him and find our hurry has only delayed us. We also give in to anxiety when we multiply our fears with wild imaginations. Always thinking the worst makes us irrational and afraid, like a child hearing noises in his closet or monsters under her bed. Our imaginations run wild in the midst of tough times, and the resulting fear paralyzes us. Multiplying makes us fearful.

*We worry when we divide life into the secular and the sacred.* God doesn't want us to compartmentalize our lives. He wants every aspect brought under His control. Selective trust makes us forget His everyday provisions. The less we include Him in our daily lives, the more anxious we become. How easy it is to tell ourselves that *this* part is in the realm of God's concern but not *that*. Wrong! Dividing life into sacred and secular categories makes us forget His presence in every area. Dividing makes us forgetful.

Take a good look through the current events of your life. What has you anxious? No matter what you are facing, worrying will do you more harm than good.

After my older sister, Luci, graduated from college, she took a job as the field representative for a school, which meant she frequently had to travel alone. And one night, about dusk, she was driving in a rural area. She noticed some lights behind her. After glancing in the rearview mirror, she realized she was being followed by a man. She thought, *Well, it's not the time I planned to stop, but I will for safety's sake.*

She pulled into a little motel and checked in at the office. Then she noticed out the glass that the man following her had parked on the side of the road, waiting for her to choose the room in this motel — one of the kind built in the shape of a horseshoe. And fear seized her. She had no weapon to protect herself. She didn't know what to say or do.

So she quickly got back into her car and pulled around the gravel driveway and into the space in front of room number eight. She got out, hurriedly set her things inside, and turned every lock on the door. And she heard the sound of his wheels coming around.

The hair stood up on the back of her neck. She didn't even have a phone back then. So she had no way to contact anybody.

She thought, *I'll get a quick shower and go to bed, and it'll all be better.* And she had gotten ready for her shower when she realized she'd left some things she needed on the bed, so she wrapped a towel around herself and walked over to get those things. As she did, she noticed that the venetian blind was cocked open. And she knew he was out there.

Every time I tell this story, I try to imagine what she must have felt like. She told me, "My eyes burst into tears in fear. But then I turned and I saw something on the glass on top of the bureau. Someone who had stayed there previously had slipped a little 3 x 5 card under the glass." Luci stopped and read,

> Come unto Me, all who are weary and
> heavy-laden, and I will give you rest.
> Take My yoke upon you, and learn from
> Me, for I am meek and lowly in heart, and
> you shall find rest for your soul. My yoke
> is easy, My burden is light. Signed, Jesus.

She said, "I grabbed that card and I showed that card to that venetian blind. And I walked over and popped that thing, went back in the bathroom and took my shower. Went to bed that night and slept like a baby." Luci knew then and there that the Lord was with her, no matter what happened.

Isn't that amazing? A few statements from Jesus and her whole frame of mind changed. Now, I am not suggesting that any time you're in danger, you should do nothing but sit on your hands and pray. You pray about it. You do all you reasonably can do to take care of yourself in your situation. Then you hand it over.

# From Anxiety to Peace

We can make a choice about what to do with our anxiety. We can carry it with us to an early grave. Or we can say, "Lord, I give this all to You, and I rest it in Your care. I have come to the cross with my greatest burden. Now I bring You all the other little ones that have been taking too much of my time and energy. And I give them all to You."

Are you worried about tomorrow? Are you getting strangled on anxieties that you can't dislodge? Do you feel like Martha, preoccupied with too many things when only one thing matters? Jesus invites you to "look at the birds, free and unfettered," and notice that they are "careless in the care of God" (Matthew 6:26 MSG). Be honest; don't you think God cares more about you than wrens or sparrows or crows?

So trust. And pray. Replace all the mental monsters of worry about tomorrow . . . or next week . . . or next month. In their place offer your fear to Him and think on true thoughts: God is in control. God cares for you. And God specializes in guarding the door of your mind, keeping out the monsters as He fills your inner world with incomprehensible, enduring peace.

# My Questions and Thoughts

_____

_____

_____

_____

_____

_____

_____

_____

_____

_____

_____

_____

_____

_____

_____

_____

_____

_____

_____

_____

_____

_____

_____

_____

_____

## My Questions and Thoughts

## Chapter 4

# You Can Find Freedom from Anxiety

### You Are Here

In her charming poem "Fifteen, Maybe Sixteen, Things to Worry About," Judith Viorst concludes with lines that ring true:

> The world could maybe come to an end
>     on next Tuesday.
> The ceiling could maybe come crashing
>     on my head.
> I maybe could run out of things for me
>     to worry about.
> And then I'd have to do my homework
>     instead.[1]

Like the child in the poem, most of us would rather worry than do something productive. And it's not all child's play when it comes to real-life situations. Consider one woman's cares:

> I now go to sleep every night with a knot in my stomach. There are just so many things in my life that I don't have any control over. My husband's company is laying people off left and right, and I don't know how we'd manage if he were out of work for any amount of time. He hates to even talk about it, and

it's driving a wedge between us. I have several nagging health problems that the doctor can't solve. And my kids—how in the world can I keep them from messing up their lives, with all the drugs and immorality and danger out there? We can't afford to send them to a Christian school. I know Christians aren't sup-posed to feel like this. But no matter how many times a day I "cast my cares upon Him," they just keep coming back!

Although we say that God is able to carry our burdens, we shoulder them until their weight drags us to the ground.

# Facing Our Captors

Worry certainly gives our active minds something to chew on, as does fear. And then anxiety comes along and eats away at our spirit. Even more damaging—together they steal our trust in God one thought at a time.

*Fear* is the emotion of alarm in reaction to a perceived danger or threat. The danger may be real (the shadow of a burglar, a rapidly approaching car) or it may be imaginary (a shutter creaking in the breeze, a scary scene in a movie), but the perception is real and defined. Fear is in the same "family" as anxiety, yet the two are different.

*Anxiety* is a more general feeling of uneasiness, a vague perception of threat. Like a low-grade fever, it can wear out the body by keeping it on a constant level of alertness. Fear brings on a rush of adrenaline; anxiety is like a slow drip of adrenaline. When alertness is called for, this ready-to-react adrenaline provides energy and creativity, but sustained in excess over the long haul, it strains both mind and body.

Anxiety can come from the perception of either an outside threat or an inner conflict. For example, a woman may feel anxiety when she drives past a place she associates with painful memories of rejection. On the other hand, a woman who desires a deeper relationship with someone but who fears rejection if she reveals her thoughts experiences anxiety.

*Worry*, however, is not a feeling. Worry is the mental action of ruminating on conflicts or fears, mulling over them, and contemplating worst-case scenarios. This reaction to anxiety serves only to increase it. Worry is an unproductive form of problem-solving because it is applied to things that can't be changed or avoided by wishing them so.

God intended for us to be free. He gave us minds to think freely, hearts to love freely, and wills to act freely. The irony, however, is that in exercising our freedom, we've imprisoned ourselves behind the bars of wrong choices and addictions, including anxiety and worry.

**How do you typically cope with fear?**

_____

_____

_____

_____

**Recall childhood experiences of fear. How did your parents or caregivers teach you to respond to these dangers (real or perceived) or handle your fear?**

_____

_____

_____

_____

**How do you think God views your fear? Your anxiety?**

_____

_____

_____

_____

 ### Discovering the Way

The prison bars of anxiety are thick and strong, and breaking free is no easy task. We need someone with a key to unlock our dank cell. Fortunately, there is such a one—Jesus Christ.

# $\mathcal{E}$mbracing $O$ur $\mathcal{E}$mancipator

God promised that the Messiah would "proclaim liberty to captives / And freedom to prisoners" (Isaiah 61:1). Freedom and liberty—two of the greatest gifts ever given—sum up Jesus's mission.

The Israelites in Old Testament times often knew literal, physical bondage and exile. Waiting seven and a half centuries for the fulfillment of Isaiah's promise must have made the dream of a messiah seem hopeless. But on an ordinary Sabbath, in a dusty little village in Israel, a man named Jesus stood in His boyhood synagogue, unrolled the scroll to Isaiah 61, and read His commission: "He has sent Me to proclaim release to the captives . . . to set free those who are oppressed" (Luke 4:18). After giving the scroll back to the attendant, Jesus sat down and announced, "Today this Scripture has been fulfilled in your hearing" (4:21).

The hometown folks didn't know what to make of this announcement. They'd seen Jesus grow up in Joseph's shop—the son of an ordinary carpenter (4:22). Throughout Jesus's ministry, very few understood the reality of His mission: to proclaim that His death and resurrection would break the bondage of sin and truly set us free — "free indeed" (John 8:36).

How have you responded to Christ's offer of freedom? Sadly, many of us have chosen to keep living behind the prison bars we've forged ourselves, confirming the truth of eighteenth-century philosopher Jean-Jacques Rousseau's observation about humans being born free yet "everywhere in chains." [2]

**Are you imprisoned by worry, fear, or anxiety? On the prison bars below, write the people, situations, or other things that evoke inner turmoil.**

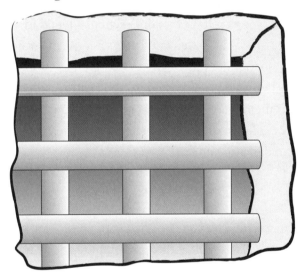

**How do fear or anxiety affect your outlook on life? Do you tend toward cheerfulness or gloominess? How does worry affect your relationships? Your health?**

_____

_____

_____

_____

_____

Mark 4:7, 18–19 presents a vivid picture of the consequences of anxiety. Have you noticed any of these qualities in your spiritual life? If so, which ones?

_____

_____

_____

_____

_____

Trouble, fear, cares, and the associated nail-biting and stress headaches—these weigh us down. And in Jesus's famous Sermon on the Mount, he addressed the problem of worry. In fact, in one section—found in Matthew 6:25–34—we read that Jesus used the word *worry* no fewer than five times. A background check reveals that its origins are tied to the meaning of being pulled "in different directions" or being "distract[ed]." [3] We are pulled in different directions, distracted from the truth and focused on fear.

## A Better Way

If we're worried, we can't be filled with peace, can we? Let's take a closer look at this passage to see how God wants us to handle our worries.

Read Matthew 6:25–34. Verses 25–26 assure us that God cares for us more than He does the birds of the air. What do we learn from this about God's view of our difficulties?

_____

_____

_____

_____

**According to verse 27, what does worry accomplish?**

_____

_____

_____

**What does worrying indicate about the worrier's view of God?**

_____

_____

_____

**Skim back over Matthew 6:25–34. In your own words, list the promises Jesus made in this passage.**

_____

_____

_____

_____

_____

**What did Jesus say to do instead of worry?**

_____

_____

_____

_____

Worry, according to Jesus, leads to four consequences. First, our value system gets confused (Matthew 6:25), turning basic needs of life into the reason or purpose for life. Second, we become selfish (6:31), utterly consumed with food, drink, and clothing. Third, our Christian distinctiveness gets blurred (6:32); we act more like unbelievers—who have nowhere to turn for help—than children of our heavenly Father, who takes care of our needs. Finally, we dread the future (Matthew 6:34). We fret over the dawning of the sun in the morning, even before the sun has set at night.

**Read the following passages from Proverbs, and contrast the positive and negative ideas in each one.**

| Proverb | Positive | Negative |
|---------|----------|----------|
| 15:13 | | |
| 15:15 | | |
| 17:22 | | |

In Philippians 4:6–7, we read that the apostle Paul exhorted believers to pray when they found themselves overcome by worry:

> Be anxious for nothing, but in every-
> thing by prayer and supplication with
> thanksgiving let your requests be made
> known to God. And the peace of God,
> which surpasses all comprehension,
> will guard your hearts and your minds
> in Christ Jesus.

**When we pray about our anxieties, how should we pray?**

_____

_____

_____

_____

When we worry, we are trying to solve our own problems rather than trusting God to take care of them. Why do you think our default reaction is to rely on ourselves instead of praying?

_____

_____

_____

_____

What promise do we have if we replace our anxieties with thankful prayers?

_____

_____

_____

_____

## Starting Your Journey

Paul Tillich said we live in an "age of anxiety."[4] And every generation could claim his little phrase as its own. Jesus could have used Tillich's words to describe the generation living in the first century, and the phrase has characterized every generation since. Look around you and you'll see a world consumed with worry, anxiety, and fear. Jesus greatly desires to set women free from these. So He offered a profound statement in a simple, encouraging command: "Do not worry" (Matthew 6:31). This, of course, is easier said than done, but if we take Jesus at His word and come to grips with worry's stranglehold, we can apply God's solution, correct our perspective, and soon discover that the door of our cell is open wide.

As we have seen in Philippians 4, Christ-followers are to worry about nothing, pray about everything. When we do so, we have joy, and we also learn to experience God's peace (Philippians 4:7). Besides praying, we're exhorted to let our gentleness be known (4:5). The phrase translated as "gentleness" is the Greek word *epieikes*—"yielding [and] kind."[5] Imagine having an easygoing sweetness to your temperament, treating others with patience and kindness, giving the Lord time to work in their lives, and yielding when everyone else is jockeying for position.

**What does Ephesians 4:31–32 command us to put away and to put into practice?**

| Put Away | Put into Practice |
|---|---|
|  |  |
|  |  |
|  |  |
|  |  |

**Describe a past or present situation in which anxiety caused you to exhibit some of the traits in Ephesians 4:31.**

_____

_____

_____

_____

_____

_____

Describe a past or present situation in which you exhibited some of the traits in Ephesians 4:32, in spite of your anxiety.

_____

_____

_____

_____

_____

What do you think accounted for the difference in your response?

_____

_____

_____

_____

_____

We could summarize Philippians 4:6–7 as, "Worry about nothing; pray about everything." If you do that, you can rest easy, as if God is saying, "Shhh." God's incomprehensible *shalom*, His peace, will guard your heart and mind like a sentry barring anxiety from entering—a sentry of peace stationed there by Christ Jesus, the One who sets us free from worry.

How have you used prayer in the past to combat your anxieties? What has been the result?

_____

_____

_____

_____

_____

**If your worries keep growing, maybe your view of God is shrinking. What traits of God's character prove His power and His faithfulness?**

_____

_____

_____

_____

_____

As we saw earlier, God's therapy for anxiety is simple: worry about nothing; pray about everything. When our focus shifts from our problems to His greatness, we are set free from our prison of distressing fear. We can rejoice, relax, and rest.

## *Perspective Matters*

Anxiety is sure to bark at us to return to our cells, like a police dog cornering a suspect. How can we keep it at bay? We continue to pray, of course, and we can also correct our perspective in three critical areas.

First, we can clean up our thinking by feeding our minds with praiseworthy thoughts (Philippians 4:8). Regardless of our difficulties, disappointments, or heartaches, if we deliberately fill our minds with true, honorable, and godly thoughts, we'll starve worry into a weakling who can be defeated.

**Using Philippians 4:8 as a guide, write one specific thought or promise you can dwell on each day this week. You may choose a Scripture for each one, come up with an inspirational saying or proverb, or design an image or picture that reflects the concept. Be creative.**

True: _____

_____

Honorable: _____

_____

Right: _____

_____

Pure: _____

_____

Lovely: _____

_____

Reputable: _____

_____

Excellent: _____

_____

Praiseworthy: _____

_____

Second, we can follow godly examples by focusing our attention on encouraging models. In Philippians 4:9, Paul told his readers to imitate him. On the surface it may appear that Paul was bragging, but he wasn't. He had been set free from the prison of worry, and through the power of the Holy Spirit, he lived a life of joy, gentleness, and peace. Paul simply offered himself as an example of what Christ can do to free us from worry.

**Whom could you follow as an encouraging model of living freely (maybe someone you know, a person in the Bible, or someone you've read about in a biography)?**

_____

_____

_____

**What, specifically, makes this person such a good example for you?**

_____

_____

_____

_____

_____

_____

**What specific action can you take this week to follow her or his example?**

_____

_____

_____

_____

_____

_____

Next, we can adjust our spiritual eyesight by finding God's peace in every circumstance (Philippians 4:9). Worry forces us to focus on the wrong things: ourselves, our circumstances, our unknown future. We can refocus and claim God's peace in every circumstance.

**Describe a situation that's causing you to struggle with worry today.**

_____

_____

_____

_____

_____

**Write a prayer asking God to give you peace in this situation.**

**Dear God,**

_____

_____

_____

_____

_____

_____

_____

Every prisoner of worry needs freedom from her self-made prison. And there is hope. It is embodied in the person and work of Jesus Christ—the Great Emancipator!

Are you locked behind the bars of anxiety? Remember to pray for, to think about, and to claim God's peace. Christ will set you free and guard your heart and mind from the temptation of worry.

**Do you really believe Jesus will set you free? If so, personalize John 8:36 and John 14:27 by writing them in your own words and inserting your name, where appropriate.**

**John 8:36**

_____

_____

_____

_____

**John 14:27**

_____

_____

_____

_____

"If the Son makes you free, you will be free indeed" (John 8:36). These words ring with joy and hope for those locked behind the prison bars of anxiety. Go ahead, push on your cell door; it's unlocked. Step out into the sunshine of freedom. Live free of care. Rejoice. Relax. Rest. Replace anxiety with prayer, thanksgiving, and laughter, and remember: "[s]he who laughs . . . lasts!"[6]

## My Questions and Thoughts

# My Questions and Thoughts

# How to Begin a Relationship with God

The Bible is the most marvelous book in the world, and it is the true Life-Map that marks the path to God. This map tells us not only how to avoid pitfalls and how to navigate the sudden roadblocks in life, but it also reveals how to enjoy the journey to the fullest. How? It points us to God—our ultimate destination. It tells us how we can come to know God Himself. Let's look at four vital truths the Scriptures reveal.

## Our Spiritual Condition: Totally Corrupt

The first truth is rather personal. One look in the mirror of Scripture, and our human condition becomes painfully clear:

> There is none righteous, not even one;
> There is none who understands,
> There is none who seeks for God;
> All have turned aside, together they
>     have become useless;
> There is none who does good,
> There is not even one.
> (Romans 3:10–12)

We are all sinners through and through—totally corrupt. Now, that doesn't mean we've committed every atrocity known to humankind. We're not as *bad* as we can be, just as *bad off* as we can be. Sin colors all our thoughts, motives, words, and actions.

Look around. Everything around us bears the smudge marks of our sinful nature. Despite our best efforts to create a perfect world, crime statistics continue to soar, divorce rates keep climbing, and families keep crumbling.

Something has gone terribly wrong in our society and in ourselves, something deadly. Contrary to how the world would repackage it, "me first" living doesn't equal rugged individuality and freedom; it equals death. As Paul said in his letter to the Romans, "The wages of sin is death" (Romans 6:23)—our emotional and physical death through sin's destructiveness, and our spiritual death from God's righteous judgment of our sin. This brings us to the second truth: God's character.

## God's Character: Infinitely Holy

How can God judge each of us for a sinful state we were born into? Our total depravity is only half the answer. The other half is God's infinite holiness.

The fact that we know things are not as they should be points us to a standard of goodness beyond ourselves. Our sense of injustice in life on this side of eternity implies a perfect standard of justice beyond our reality. That standard and source is God Himself. And God's standard of holiness contrasts starkly with our sinful condition.

Scripture says that "God is Light, and in Him there is no darkness at all" (1 John 1:5). He is absolutely holy—which creates a problem for us. If He is so pure, how can we who are so impure relate to Him?

Perhaps we could try being better people, try to tilt the balance in favor of our good deeds, or seek out wisdom and knowledge for self-improvement. Throughout history, people have attempted to live up to God's standard by keeping the Ten Commandments or living by their own code of ethics. Unfortunately, no one can come close to satisfying the demands of God's law. Romans 3:20 says, "By the works of the Law no flesh will be justified in His sight; for through the Law comes the knowledge of sin."

## Our Need: A Substitute

So here we are: sinners by nature and sinners by choice, trying to pull ourselves up by our own bootstraps and attain a relationship with our holy Creator. But every time we try, we fall flat on our faces. We can't live a good enough life to make up for our sin, because God's standard isn't "good enough"—it's *perfection*. And we can't make amends for the offense our sin has created without dying for it.

Who can get us out of this mess?

If someone could live perfectly, honoring God's law, and would bear sin's death penalty for us—in our place—then we would be saved from our predicament. But is there such a person? Thankfully, yes!

Meet your substitute—*Jesus Christ*. He is the One who took death's place for you!

> [God] made [Jesus Christ] who knew
> no sin to be sin on our behalf, so that
> we might become the righteousness of
> God in Him. (2 Corinthians 5:21)

## God's Provision: A Savior

God rescued us by sending His Son, Jesus, to die for our sins on the cross (1 John 4:9–10). Jesus was fully human and fully divine (John 1:1, 18), a truth that ensures His understanding of our weaknesses, His power to forgive, and His ability to bridge the gap between God and us (Romans 5:6–11). In short, we are "justified as a gift by His grace through the redemption which is in Christ Jesus" (3:24). Two words in this verse bear further explanation: *justified* and *redemption*.

*Justification* is God's act of mercy, in which He declares righteous the believing sinners while we are still in our sinning state. Justification doesn't mean that God *makes* us righteous, so that we never sin again, rather that He *declares* us righteous—much like a judge pardons a guilty criminal. Because Jesus took our sin upon Himself and suffered our judgment on the cross, God forgives our debt and proclaims us PARDONED.

*Redemption* is Christ's act of paying the complete price to release us from sin's bondage. God sent His Son to bear His wrath for all of our sins—past, present, and future (Romans 3:24–26; 2 Corinthians 5:21). In humble obedience, Christ willingly endured the shame of the cross for our sake (Mark 10:45; Romans 5:6–8; Philippians 2:8). Christ's death satisfied God's righteous demands. He no longer holds our sins against us, because His own Son paid the penalty for them. We are freed from the slave market of sin, never to be enslaved again!

# Placing Your Faith in Christ

These four truths describe how God has provided a way to Himself through Jesus Christ. Since the price has been paid in full by God, we must respond to His free gift of eternal life in total faith and confidence in Him to save us. We must step forward into the relationship with God that He has prepared for us—not by doing good works or by being a good person, but by coming to Him just as we are and accepting His justification and redemption by faith.

> For by grace you have been saved through faith; and that not of yourselves, it is the gift of God; not as a result of works, so that no one may boast. (Ephesians 2:8–9)

We accept God's gift of salvation simply by placing our faith in Christ alone for the forgiveness of our sins. Would you like to enter a relationship with your Creator by trusting in Christ as your Savior? If so, here's a simple prayer you can use to express your faith:

> *Dear God,*
>
> *I know that my sin has put a barrier between You and me. Thank You for sending Your Son, Jesus, to die in my place. I trust in Jesus alone to forgive my sins, and I accept His gift of eternal life. I ask Jesus to be my personal Savior and the Lord of my life. Thank You. In Jesus's name I pray, amen.*

If you've prayed this prayer or one like it and you wish to find out more about knowing God and His plan for you in the Bible, contact us at Insight for Living. Our contact information is on page 73.

The next time you study a road map, remember the One who created the perfect plan for your life, and remind yourself that you know Him personally. Rejoice in His indescribable gift!

# $\mathscr{E}$ndnotes

## Opening Quote

1. Alister E. McGrath, *The Journey: A Pilgrim in the Lands of the Spirit*, 1st ed. (New York: Doubleday, 2000), 21–22.

## Chapter 1

1. Maurice E. Wagner, *The Sensation of Being Somebody: Building an Adequate Self-Concept* (Grand Rapids: Zondervan, 1975), 32.

2. Wagner, *The Sensation of Being Somebody*, 165.

3. Wagner, *The Sensation of Being Somebody*, 164–67.

## Chapter 2

1. James Dobson, *What Wives Wish Their Husbands Knew about Women* (Wheaton, Ill.: Living Books: Tyndale, 1987), 22–23. Used by permission.

2. Maurice E. Wagner, *The Sensation of Being Somebody: Building an Adequate Self-Concept* (Grand Rapids: Zondervan, 1975), 162.

3. Robert C. Roberts, *Taking the Word to Heart: Self and Other in an Age of Therapies* (Grand Rapids: Eerdmans, 1993), 23.

4. Wagner, *The Sensation of Being Somebody*, 167.

5. Donald P. Regier, "A Chosen Child: The Mystery of Adoption," *Kindred Spirit* (Summer 1997), 6.

6. Dobson, *What Wives Wish Their Husbands Knew About Women*, 35. Used by permission.

## Chapter 3

1. W. E. Vine, *An Expository Dictionary of New Testament Words* (Old Tappan, N.J.: Fleming H. Revell, 1966), 168.

2. Peter Marshall, quoted in Catherine Marshall, ed., *The Prayers of Peter Marshall* (New York: McGraw-Hill, 1954), 36.

# Chapter 4

1. Judith Viorst, "Fifteen, Maybe Sixteen, Things to Worry About," in *If I Were in Charge of the World and Other Worries* (New York: Atheneum Books, 1981), 7.

2. Jean-Jacques Rousseau, *The Social Contract*, trans. Maurice Cranston (New York: Penguin Books, 1968), 49.

3. W. E. Vine, *An Expository Dictionary of New Testament Words* (Old Tappan, N.J.: Fleming H. Revell, 1966), 168.

4. Paul Tillich, *The Courage to Be* (New Haven, Conn.: Yale University Press, 1966), 35.

5. Frederick William Danker, ed., *A Greek-English Lexicon of the New Testament and Other Early Christian Literature*, 3d rev. ed. (Chicago: University of Chicago Press, 2000), 371.

6. Erma Bombeck, "Motherhood—Love and Laughter," in *Forever, Erma: Best-Loved Writing from America's Favorite Humorist* (New York: Guideposts, 1996), 19.

# Resources for Probing Further

For further information on anxiety and self worth, here are a few resources we would like to recommend. Of course, we cannot always endorse everything a writer or ministry says, so we encourage you to approach these and all other non-biblical resources with wisdom and discernment.

Backus, William, and Marie Chapian. *Telling Yourself the Truth: Find Your Way Out of Depression, Anxiety, Fear, Anger, and Other Common Problems by Applying the Principles of Misbelief Therapy.* Minneapolis: Bethany House, 2000.

DeMoss, Nancy Leigh. *Lies Women Believe and the Truth that Sets Them Free.* Chicago: Moody, 2001.

Dillow, Linda. *Calm My Anxious Heart: A Woman's Guide to Finding Contentment.* Colorado Springs: NavPress, 2007.

George, Elizabeth. *Understanding Your Blessings in Christ.* Eugene, Ore.: Harvest House, 2008.

Hunt, June. *Seeing Yourself through God's Eyes: A 31-Day Devotional Guide.* Eugene, Ore.: Harvest House, 2008.

McGee, Robert S. *The Search for Significance: Seeing Your True Worth Through God's Eyes.* Nashville: Thomas Nelson, 2003.

Phillips, Bob. *Overcoming Anxiety and Depression: Practical Tools to Help You Deal with Negative Emotions.* Eugene, Ore.: Harvest House, 2007.

Swindoll, Charles R. *Come Before Winter and Share My Hope.* Grand Rapids: Zondervan, 1985.

Swindoll, Charles R. *Encouraging Words for Discouraging Days.* Compact disc series. Plano, Tex.: Insight for Living, 2008.

Swindoll, Charles R. *Facing Life's Problems with God's Hope.* Compact disc series. Plano, Tex.: Insight for Living, 2003.

Swindoll, Charles R. *Getting through the Tough Stuff: It's Always Something!* Nashville: Thomas Nelson, 2004.

Swindoll, Charles R. *God's Provision in Time of Need.* Nashville: Thomas Nelson, 1997.

# We Are Here for You

If you desire to find out more about knowing God and His plan for you in the Bible, contact us. Insight for Living provides staff pastors who are available for free written correspondence or phone consultation. These seminary-trained and seasoned counselors have years of experience and are well-qualified guides for your spiritual journey.

Please feel welcome to contact your regional Pastoral Ministries by using the information below:

## United States

Insight for Living
Pastoral Ministries
Post Office Box 269000
Plano, Texas 75026-9000
USA
972-473-5097, Monday through Friday,
8:00 a.m. – 5:00 p.m. Central time
www.insight.org/contactapastor

## Canada

Insight for Living Canada
Pastoral Ministries
Post Office Box 2510
Vancouver, BC V6B 3W7
CANADA
1-800-663-7639
info@insightforliving.ca

## Australia, New Zealand, and South Pacific

Insight for Living Australia
Pastoral Care
Post Office Box 1011
Bayswater, VIC 3153
AUSTRALIA
1 300 467 444

## United Kingdom and Europe

Insight for Living United Kingdom
Pastoral Care
Post Office Box 348
Leatherhead
KT22 2DS
UNITED KINGDOM
0800 915 9364
+44 (0) 1372 370 055
pastoralcare@insightforliving.org.uk

# Ordering Information

If you would like to order additional *LifeMaps* or other Insight for Living resources, please contact the ministry location that serves you.

## United States

Insight for Living
Post Office Box 269000
Plano, Texas 75026-9000
USA
1-800-772-8888
Monday through Friday,
7:00 a.m. – 7:00 p.m.
Central time
www.insight.org
www.insightworld.org

## Canada

Insight for Living Canada
Post Office Box 2510
Vancouver, BC V6B 3W7
CANADA
1-800-663-7639
www.insightforliving.ca

## Australia, New Zealand, and South Pacific

Insight for Living Australia
Post Office Box 1011
Bayswater, VIC 3153
AUSTRALIA
1 300 467 444
www.insight.asn.au

## United Kingdom and Europe

Insight for Living United Kingdom
Post Office Box 348
Leatherhead
KT22 2DS
UNITED KINGDOM
0800 915 9364
www.insightforliving.org.uk

## Other International Locations

International constituents may contact the U.S. office
through our Web site (www.insightworld.org), mail
queries, or by calling +1-972-473-5136.